THE CHOICE IS YOURS.

THAT IS THE CORE PHILOSOPHY OF THE MINDFUL LIFE COLLECTION CREATED BY JAE ELLARD. The choice is yours to start anywhere, at any point in your life, to create more awareness around the choices you make each day that either support or sabotage your desired outcome to create meaningful engagement and sustainable balance between the interconnected roles, relationships, and responsibilities that make up your life.

The Mindful Life collection includes four books to generate awareness, reflection, and conversation.

Stop & Think: Creating New Awareness is about the choices you have and your understanding of the impact of those choices.

Stop & See: Developing Intentional Habits is about your ability to consciously choose to create habits that support your definitions of balance and success.

Stop & Listen: Practicing Presence is about working with your choices to create deeper engagement with self, others, and your environment.

Beyond Tips & Tricks: Mindful Management is about leading groups to take accountability for making and accepting choices.

ARE YOU A MINDFUL MANAGER?

That is the question this book will explore. You will learn what it actually means to be a mindful manager and how managers can lead groups to take accountability for making and accepting choices that either support or sabotage a person's ability to create meaningful engagement and sustainable balance. Through this content, you will understand your ability as a manager to intentionally create a connected, conscious, engaged organization.

To better understand
what it means to be a mindful manager,
it's helpful to start with the concept of balance.

WHY START WITH BALANCE?

Regardless of how you feel about this topic, the impact of imbalance has become one of the core issues most managers face today.

Mindful management starts with balance because the topic is the confluence for how people engage at work, combining work-life balance, workload balance and energy balance.

This includes the need to create flexibility in location and work hours for your team, navigating a sea of technological devices to stay connected, balancing more work requests with fewer resources, and at the same time building morale, inspiring great work and maintaining a healthy work environment so your team can sustain the new normal of modern-day "busy."

WHAT IS THIS THING CALLED BALANCE?

As a manager, you are well aware that when it comes to this topic, there is no shortage of opinions about what balance means, how to address it, and the impact it has on individuals and teams around the world.

In fact, the term "work-life balance" lends itself to much debate (sometimes heated debate), and many people choose to rename the concept using terms such as harmony, integration, blur, or flexibility – or even ignore it altogether.

There are many ways to talk about balance and issues that surround it, but only one way that feels right for you as a manager.

The good news is that although people around the world may use different words to describe what balance means to them, most people share a similar desired outcome, **which is to create easy joy and meaningful engagement between the interconnected relationships, roles, and responsibilities that make up life.**

It's absolutely okay that balance means different things to different people and that different people call it different things. Accepting that it is different for everyone and having conversations about what it means and how it manifests is at the core of being a mindful manager.

TALKING ABOUT "BALANCE" CAN BE A CHALLENGE.

As a manager, balance is a rather complex topic to discuss with your team, your leaders, and your peers. (And not just because balance means different things to different people.)

Most times it's because the conversations are not being had. Or if they are, the conversation gets weighed down in the pain points –the effect imbalance is having on the team or on the individual (or both). When a conversation is focused on the pain points, people get stuck on venting about all the impacts – things like workload, disengagement, too much email, too many meetings, limited resources, unclear boundaries, or not enough time to accomplish tasks. This creates a situation that makes it hard for you as a manager to identify or address the root cause of the pain points.

Many managers report that they avoid talking about the impact that imbalance, especially the volume and intensity of work, is having on their team and how work is getting done, simply because they are unsure of how to have the conversation and where to even start the conversation. Managers also share that they avoid having these conversations because they don't really want to know the extent of the impact, because they are afraid of learning too much, or because they don't know how to support the team or the individual.

This combination of challenges creates a situation of perpetual imbalance and, in some cases, disengagement for the team because the conversation gets stuck in an endless loop focused on pain points.

Teams and organizations get stuck because the pain is real, the cause is unclear, and most managers don't have (or don't think they have) the capacity or time to have conversations that go beyond the pain points. This results in teams staying stuck in an imbalance loop, with managers feeding the pain points one at a time with simple tips and tricks to try to ease the greatest pain of the moment.

In the past, organizations have not provided much (if any) guidance, training, or structure to managers for how to break the imbalance loop and have mindful conversations in a way that addresses the underlying causes and moves people to action and accountability for their own choices.

IMBALANCE IS LIKE A COLD.

To address the issues surrounding imbalance, most companies and leaders are focused on fixing the pain points – the symptoms of the cold – as opposed to preventing the cold from spreading.

When a company or team first becomes aware that it is experiencing the impact of imbalance, the first action in most cases is to invest in developing (or promoting) employee benefits to address the symptoms. Unfortunately, this does not always work. It can certainly help in some cases, but does not address the systemic causes.

There is no dispute that balance-focused benefits can help support employees; however, unless the conversation shifts to the systemic causes, these types of benefits will not be enough to retain and attract top talent and create sustainable, positive, and productive work environments.

Being a mindful manager begins by shifting your perception from treating symptoms to prevention.

A team that is out of balance is like a team with a cold. If your team had a cold, of course you want to address the symptoms they are experiencing, but you also want to address the causes. You want to learn why they are getting a cold, how to reduce the frequency in which they have colds, and how to prevent a cold from spreading across the team.

THE WAY TO BREAK THE CYCLE AND MOVE
FROM TREATING SYMPTOMS TO PREVENTION
IS THROUGH HAVING MINDFUL CONVERSATIONS.

MINDFUL
CONVERSATIONS

WHAT IS A MINDFUL CONVERSATION?

Most company training programs prepare you as a manager to engage in specific types of conversations with your team – for example, you are taught how to have a conversation to provide feedback or give performance reviews. Scripted, formatted conversations don't work when it comes to managing issues related to balance, because each team, each person, each manager is different.

As a manager, the conversation needs to stem from what is true for you when it comes to communicating expectations, setting boundaries, and addressing energy, the core elements that create and maintain balance at both the individual and team level.

> A mindful conversation is when you make the content of your message as authentic as possible with clear intent.

MINDFUL CONVERSATION

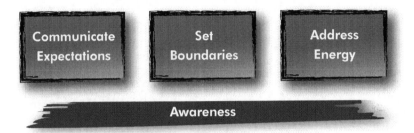

The practice of mindful management is about choosing to
discuss issues you might not have ever considered discussing openly with your team until now. These issues includes
conversations around prioritization, pushing back, volume of
workload, value of work produced, flexible work arraignments,
working weekends/evenings, or working in environments that
feel awkward or stressful. By initiating a mindful conversation,
you can create an intentional, proactive dialogue around these
and other pain points associated with workplace imbalance.

AWARENESS

AWARENESS IS THE ABILITY TO SEE THE WORLD AND HOW YOU SHOW UP IN IT.

MINDFUL CONVERSATIONS BEGIN WITH AWARENESS

Awareness is the ability to see the world and how you show up in it. Why is this important? If you are unable to see how you and your team are showing up, you will be unable to have mindful conversations about the underlying cause of pain points the team is facing, and you will be stuck triaging them with an endless parade of tips and tricks.

Before you can begin to have mindful conversations, you must have the willingness to really see what is going on.

In the case of being a mindful manager, awareness means the ability to see your team, their behaviors, and the impact their behaviors have on each other, business partners, customers, and business outcomes, as well as the impact YOUR behavior is having on them.

Because whether you are aware of it or not, all behavior (yours and your team) has an impact and there is a result, whether intentional or unintentional. That is the underlying philosophy for the Mindful Life program called The Awareness Framework.

THE AWARENESS FRAMEWORK

Behavior has an impact and there is a result, whether intentional or unintentional, related to the behavior. When people choose to, or are empowered to, become more aware of their behavior, they are able to be more accountable in their roles and to their teams, more authentic in their communication, and more awake in their environment (both literally and figuratively). The impact to the team and organization is a shift in the team's ability to be more innovative and more productive on multiple levels. The result is sustainable success for both the organization and the employee.

THE AWARENESS FRAMEWORK

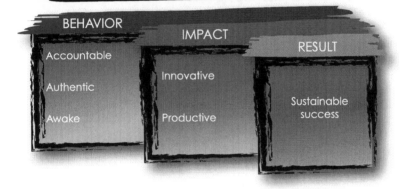

BEHAVIOR

Accountable

Authentic

Awake

IMPACT

Innovative

Productive

RESULT

Sustainable success

Awareness around the impact of YOUR behavior as a manager is essential for you to understand. Intentional or not, you set the tone for how your team shows up. Do you work weekends? Do you work late at night? Do you take a vacation? Do you work from vacation? Are you disengaged in meetings? Do you block out time in your calendar for people? Do you ask the hard questions when no one else wants to? Your actions create the unspoken atmosphere under which your team operates.

Your behavior as a leader, has an impact on the people you manage, every single day, whether you are aware of it or not. This concept is also referred to as the "shadow of the leader." The good news is that becoming more aware of your behavior and the impact it has on others is a skill that can be learned.

AWARENESS IS A SKILL

The skill of awareness is important because it allows you as a manager to collect authentic information to help you make informed choices and have mindful conversations with your your team.

Just like learning math, you learn awareness in different layers that build on each other. First you have to learn addition and subtraction before you can learn multiplication and division, then you move into algebra, calculus, and statistics. You can't start learning math at a statistics level; you can try, but odds are you won't get very far.

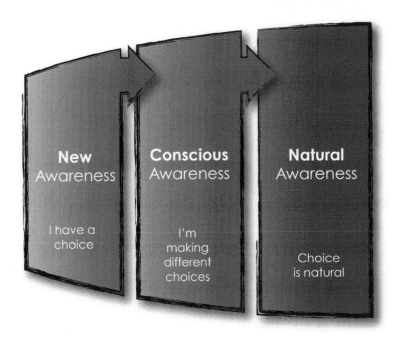

New awareness is about taking an inventory of your world and understanding the impact of your behavior on the world around you and within you – things like what makes you happy, sad, and stressed. New awareness is where you become aware you have choices.

Conscious awareness is being more conscious about what it is you are seeing around you and understanding it at a deeper level. It's the place of knowing you have choices. Some days you might make choices that sabotage your desired outcomes for balance and success, and other days you might make choices that support your desired outcomes. Both ways you choose and you are aware that it is a choice.

Natural awareness is where you fully see your behavior patterns and internalize making choices that support your desired outcome for balance and success. This is where balance has become a lifestyle or a habit and feels natural.

Keep in mind that it's simply not possible or realistic to have awareness around your team's behaviors and impacts at all times. It is possible, though, to help guide your team to create awareness around their own behaviors, and that occurs through learning, implementing, modeling the skill of awareness.

The practice of awareness is what will enable you to move beyond having tips and tricks type conversations about pain points to discussing and addressing the underlying issues that are creating imbalance for your team.

COMMUNICATE EXPECTATIONS

AN **EXPECTATION** IS A BELIEF **ABOUT THE FUTURE** THAT MAY OR MAY NOT BE REALISTIC.

WHY IS IT IMPORTANT TO TALK ABOUT EXPECTATIONS?

Expectations are everywhere in our life – at home, at work, in our relationships with others and self. They can be about anything we want or hope to have happen. Sometimes they are grounded in reality and other times they are from outer space, and many times – especially at work – they are unclear. This is because creating a two-way opportunity between managers and their team to openly share, set, and communicate expectations is not commonly done, especially around the topic of balance.

Mindful conversations about your expectations allow you to provide or receive context and clarity around purpose, needs, and outcomes.

When it comes to expectations at work, there are three ways to consider them.

TEAM: What do you expect from your team, and your team of you?

YOUR MANAGER: What does your manager expect from you, and you of your manager?

SELF: What do you expect from yourself?

When expectations are shared, everyone is on the same page. It doesn't mean everyone will agree, but it does mean everyone has the same understanding and is clear about what is expected to move forward.

TEAM EXPECTATIONS

Let's be honest: Employees LOVE to blame their managers for their imbalance, level of stress, workload, or lack of context. Not because your team members are ill meaning, but because it is much easier to blame you or maybe your manager than to take accountability for the choices they are making or ways they are working that might be the actual reason for the pain points they are experiencing.

It is not up to you to manage your employees' balance, workload, goals or commitments. It is up to you to teach them they have a choice in how they manage these things for themselves and to have ongoing conversations with them to provide guidance and that's about it.

Your job is to understand the expectations your team members have on you and you on them, and to encourage conversations for clarity when needed and as often as needed.

QUESTIONS TO ASK YOUR TEAM

Do you expect me to
* Be reachable at all times and on weekends?
* Respond to email the same day you send it?
* Know everything you are working on?
* Help with prioritizing work?
* Know your flexible work needs?

SAMPLE EXPECTATIONS TO SHARE WITH YOUR TEAM

I expect you to
* Be "on call" only when specified
* Be offline on weekends, but reachable for emergencies
* Respond to email within 24 hours
* Ask for help prioritizing
* Tell me if you need help pushing back on requests that don't relate to work goals

YOUR MANAGER'S EXPECTATIONS OF YOU

You have expectations of your team, and your manager has expectations of you. As we have discussed, having conversations around our expectations for balance and team stability is rather new, so your manager might not be proactively having these conversations with you. The good news is that you can start the conversation with your manager just as easily as you can start the conversation with your team.

It also might be possible that your organization has a companywide policy or expectation around balance, flexible work arrangements, and work-from-home policies. If you are not sure, start a conversation about it and see what is available so that you are clear if there are certain expectations on you that you need to apply to your team.

QUESTIONS TO ASK YOUR MANAGER

Do you expect me to

- Be reachable at all times and on weekends?
- Respond to email the same day you send it?
- Uphold company vacation and sick time policies?
- Communicate specific company policies about work-life balance?
- Know your flexible work needs?

SAMPLE EXPECTATIONS TO SHARE WITH YOUR MANAGER

I expect to

- Be "on call" only when specified
- Be offline on weekends, but reachable for emergencies
- Respond to email within 24 hours
- Receive your support in prioritizing and pushing back as needed for out-of-scope work requests

EXPECTATIONS ON YOURSELF

Finally, there are the expectations you have for yourself as a manager and the ideas you have around how you want to be perceived as a manager.

Many managers want to be liked by their team, which is only natural as all humans yearn for acceptance. However, there is a difference between a leader who pleases and a leader who inspires.

For you to be a mindful manager to address the impact of imbalance, it is essential that you become clear on what you expect for yourself when it comes to the topic of balance. What does balance actually mean to you? Consider if your behavior might be in or out of alignment with your definition of balance and expectations on yourself.

QUESTIONS TO ASK YOURSELF

- What does balance mean to me?
- How am I making choices that support having that type of balance?
- When it comes to balance, how do I want to be perceived by my team?
- In what ways do I want to lead by example?
- What are my flexible work needs?
- Do I want to please my team or inspire them?

SET
BOUNDARIES

A **BOUNDARY** IS A LIMIT
THAT IS SET TO **PROTECT,**
HONOR, OR **UPHOLD**
A DESIRE, VALUE, OR INTENTION.

WHY TALK ABOUT BOUNDARIES AT WORK?

Setting clear boundaries around the right issues will resolve most imbalance and engagement challenges for your team, and at the same time show by example how the team can do it for themselves with their business partners, customers, and other key stakeholders.

A core function of a manager is to lead, and setting boundaries is about leading your team to take action to create meaningful engagement and sustainable balance between the interconnected (and blurry) roles, relationships, and responsibilities of life.

> Mindful conversations about boundaries allows you to express your own limits and the ones you want to set for the team that directly relate to helping improve team and individual engagement and productivity.

At work, common boundaries are things like job descriptions, commitments, and office hours. Other boundaries that are just as common that most managers and employees don't talk openly about include working during vacation, expressing when it is okay to contact someone at night and on weekends, when and where people get their work done, how meetings are conducted, and when and where technological devices are used.

Most managers are clear what the pain points are for their team and are aware of the imbalance loop going on around them. This is great information to know, because this is how you choose what boundaries need to be established to address the root causes of imbalance for your team.

As a manager, you can choose to set as many or as few boundaries for your team as you want and they need. That said, every team can benefit from some structured, mindful conversation around common causes of imbalanced behavior that impact work outcomes.

THE FOUR BLOCKS TO ENGAGEMENT

There are four main engagement blocks that are universal to work teams that can easily be addressed through setting boundaries. The blocks differ slightly in the words used to describe the impact and scenarios in which they manifest, but the consequences to the individual and organization are the same, regardless of country, job level, or type of work.

By setting and communicating boundaries for your team around these engagement blocks, you can reduce, if not eliminate, some of the imbalance pain points teams get stuck on. There are, of course, many more boundaries you can create for your team once you have some established standards around the core engagement blocks.

1. NOT TALKING ABOUT WHAT IS HAPPENING

When teams don't talk about what is going on (change, volume of work, limited or lost resources, imbalance, and stress), then they are distracted. It could be by fear or anxiety or by the stories they and others are making up to replace conversations that are not happening.

2. STRUGGLE FOR FLEXIBILITY

Some employees need a lot of it, and others crave structure. When there are no guidelines around what flexibility means to the team, it can result in disengagement, with some people taking advantage of the benefit and others struggling to understand what is expected of them.

3. UNCLEAR DIGITAL BOUNDARIES

This is a huge trigger for disengagement in teams, both in terms of disruption that devices can cause in a day as well as understanding what tool to use and when. Tools like email, instance messaging, phone, SMS, and video conferencing (to name a few) can be overwhelming in terms of knowing when to use which tool and for what purpose.

4. MEETING DISEMPOWERMENT

Simply put, feeling disempowered in a meeting causes disengagement. This includes things like volume of meetings, meetings with no agenda, poor follow-up, poorly executed meetings, and not having the right people present to make a decision.

BLOCK: NOT TALKING ABOUT WHAT IS HAPPENING

Simply put, have the conversation with your team about what is really going on.

These conversations could be about acknowledging volume of workload, fears around organizational changes, confusion about competing priorities, establishing baseline for work style preferences, setting or sharing expectations, or expressing unmet needs.

Regardless of the topic, creating a consistent space to acknowledge impacts and preferences not only helps to address issues as they occur, it works to build trust and keep communication open with the team. Even if you don't know the answers to some of their questions or are unable to accommodate some of their requests, building the opportunity for your team to be heard is at the core of practicing mindful management.

BOUNDARY: ESTABLISH CONSISTENT TEAM CONVERSATIONS

There are some simple ways to create the habit of having consistent conversations with your team around triggers of imbalance.

- Incorporate the topic (imbalance and engagement blocks) into 1:1 meetings.
- In team meetings, offer your team a chance to voice work style preferences and non-work interests.
- Share work style preferences and non-work experiences with your team.
- Let your team know what issues/blocks you are working on, so they can see you as a human with similar struggles. (This will build trust and set the tone that it's okay to discuss what is going on.)

Ask open-ended questions, such as:

- What is your biggest concern right now?
- What blocks are you facing right now that are having an impact on your ability to be engaged at work?
- What non-work goals do you have right now?
- What is important to you outside of work?

BLOCK: UNCLEAR DIGITAL BOUNDARIES

Digital devices are both a blessing and a curse – they can either support the creation of deeper engagement and efficiency or sabotage connection and productivity.

With digital flexibility essential to how work gets done, so must be standards of digital responsibility for each team. Within corporate cultures, it's the same from country to country: People struggle with their relationship with their mobile devices including phones, laptops, and tablets. Although these are all amazing technological devices, employees are often unclear on acceptable digital boundaries and how to communicate them to others.

A top struggle is defining a standard for how often to check work email (from any device) when not at work. More than that, employees struggle with which method of communication is best to use and when to use it to contact colleagues. Getting clear as a team around the acceptable uses of tools like Outlook, instant messaging, video conferencing, SMS, and voice mail is essential to help teams better support others and eliminate distraction.

BOUNDARY: SET CLEAR DIGITAL BOUNDARIES

When clear expectations and digital boundaries are set (and followed) by managers around what behaviors are acceptable, employees instantly feel more empowered to support the boundaries and use technology to its fullest and best potential.

Questions to discuss with your team are:
- What device do you prefer to use to do your work?
- After how many emails should the issue move to a meeting?
- What is an acceptable response time for emails?
- Is it okay to use SMS with work colleagues?
- What can I do when people are on their phones or laptops in meetings and I feel that they are not engaged?
- Is instant messaging the best tool for the conversation?
- Is it okay to turn instant messaging off?

BLOCK: STRUGGLE WITH FLEXIBILITY

The number one thing employees say they want is flexibility. That said, most employees have also shared that they sometimes struggle with too much flexibility in how, when, and where to work. Don't misunderstand – all employees want and demand flexibility, but most people need help learning to work within this new, highly flexible work environment.

As a manager leading a team where everyone has different needs, preferences, work styles, work locations, and even different hours, it can be a bit overwhelming to wrap your head around and maybe even frustrating to accommodate at times.

Employees say that they want the work to be about outcomes, not hours logged or time spent sitting in an assigned workspace. Employees have a deep desire for freedom and trust from management to do the work needed to get the job done. That might happen in the office, at home, on a train, or even during a vacation, which isn't always a negative if circumstances permit and proper boundaries have been established.

Regardless, it's about having the choice and support from management (you) to do it in a way that works for the individual, in a predictable, consistent way that meets the needs of the business at the same time. And no, this does not mean everyone wants to work from home; in fact, quite the opposite — they want to feel more in control of the time they do have at work and know that they can have the choice to get things done elsewhere if a situation calls for it.

BOUNDARY: DEFINE FLEXIBILITY

Essential elements to creating flexibility include work style preferences that might include location, times of day, communication tools, and evening and weekend work arrangements.

Questions to discuss with your team are:
- What does flexibility mean to you?
- What do you think is realistic to meet the needs of your job?
- Where and what hours do you prefer to work?
- Why do you need such flexibility?
- When are your work style preferences non-negotiable?

BLOCK: MEETING DISEMPOWERMENT

No matter where you work or what you do, there are many pain points associated with meetings. Common pain points include too many meetings, lack of agendas or clear outcomes, awareness on the amount of time actually needed to discuss an issue, being present in the meeting, and getting the right people together, which includes making sure the key decision maker is in the room if necessary.

It's very common that people go to meetings when they don't know why they are going, because they are fearful of pushing back, because of who might be in the meeting, or because they fear being perceived as "not a team player." Another common trend is to invite others to meetings as a defensive strategy, because it is easier to communicate in a group setting or have the fallback to say, "You were invited to the meeting where this was discussed."

Then there is the behavior that occurs in meetings, with people distracted on their devices, interrupting each other, or taking the meeting agenda in a different direction (the list could go on). The result is disengagement from work that needs to be done and between the people who need to work together to get it done.

BOUNDARY: MEETING STANDARDS

Working to ensure and communicate standards of meeting etiquette can go a long way toward driving efficiency and creating a more balanced working environment.

Questions to consider are:
* What is the best length for a meeting: 15, 30, or 45 minutes?
* When does a meeting actually need to happen? (Can it be done over email or social media sites?)
* Who really needs to be in the meeting, and what is each person's role (e.g., owner, reviewer, approver)?
* How do you want technology used in your meeting? (For example, do you have a device-down policy for anyone not presenting?)
* What do you expect to know before walking into and out of a meeting?
* What do you expect to happen after each meeting?
* How do you want each meeting to start?

ADDRESS
ENERGY

ENERGY

IS AVAILABLE

POWER

WHAT DOES IT MEAN TO ADDRESS ENERGY?

Energy can be described as a feeling you have, a charged or emotional thought you have, the way your body feels, or even the way the room feels in a meeting. You have energy. Your team has energy. The company, your family, and the world have energy. Each person's and each system's energy mingles and mixes together and has a resulting impact – sometimes positive, sometimes negative, and sometimes neutral.

As a manager, is it very important to have awareness around your own energy, to be willing to see the flow of energy of your team and, when needed, to have a conversation with your team about the impact of their energy.

> **Mindful conversations to address energy allow you to acknowledge something you feel that is occurring and creating an impact.**

This is where the skill of awareness becomes important. When you have awareness around your behaviors and some of the behaviors of your team, then you can see the impact these behaviors have in terms of the energy or lack of energy people might have, which directly impacts both the quality and quantity of work produced.

When you have the willingness to have a conversation around what you see, you are then able to calm the energy or redirect it in healthier ways for both the individual and the team.

ENERGY IMBALANCE

What human behavior specialists know about energy is that too little or too much can cause an imbalance. There are many signs of energy imbalance, some easier to see and address than others. Most times at work, these imbalances show up as stress behaviors.

Interestingly, too much or too little energy shows up the same way. Managers might notice lack of engagement, defensive behavior, poor collaboration, and ongoing health issues.

As a manager, you are in a unique position to be able to see the behavior of your team, which also means you have a choice to see where and when the energy clogs or gushes and to then have a mindful conversation about what is happening for the benefit of both the individual and the team.

This is historically another area in which managers have avoided having conversations, because it's hard to know what to say to address a charged emotional event or to deal with a situation in which people are withdrawing and repressing their emotions.

Imbalance shows up in five different energy engagement types:

1. Unable to engage
2. Underengaged
3. Overengaged
4. Enraged
5. Healthfully engaged

There are some specific conversations you as a manager can have when you observe these changes in energy across your team.

SCARCE ENERGY

Scarce energy is when individuals have too little energy, leading to behavior in which people are either unable to engage or choose to be underengaged.

UNABLE TO ENGAGE

This type of energy can take the appearance of "burnout" and is usually driven by inability to manage change and stress. Many times this person may be struggling with multiple and/ or major health issues, which results in them missing work or being distracted while at work.

WHAT YOU CAN DO:
* Initiate an authentic conversation about their state of being using phrases like:
    - I've noticed you've not been feeling well lately. Tell me what is going on.
    - It seems like the workload is having an impact on you – tell me what is going on for you.
    - What is it like for you right now?
    - What are you doing to create balance and recharge?
* Suggest short-term disability or vacation as a way to recharge
* Show an interest in their health/personal life, and suggest visiting with HR for resources
* Work closely with them to help prioritize current tasks
* Review commitments and discuss what is realistic in the current situation

UNDERENGAGED

This type of energy can take the appearance of "victim" and is usually driven by lack of clarity in roles/commitments or low self-confidence. Many times this person is totally lost and overwhelmed with the work and unable to ask for support or assistance.

WHAT YOU CAN DO:

* Initiate an authentic conversation about their state of being
  - I've noticed you've been feeling disconnected from the team lately. Tell me what's going on.
  - It seems like the workload is having an impact on you – share what's it like for you right now.
  - What is your experience with work and the team right now?
  - What are you doing to create balance and recharge?
* Refocus them on commitments and goals in and out of work
* Use a strength builder–based conversation to help them to see and own their core strengths
* Discuss with them the core of their true complaints
* Assess if they are just venting to be heard or are seeking action
* Encourage them to take a few health days off to recharge

ABUNDANT ENERGY

Abundant energy is when individuals have too much energy, which creates behaviors in which people are either overengaged or choose to be enraged.

OVERENGAGED

This type of energy can take the appearance of a "martyr" and is usually driven by fear of not being "good enough." Many times this is the person who takes it all on and is unable to do it all (or do any of it well).

WHAT YOU CAN DO:

* Initiate an authentic conversation about their state of being
    - I've noticed you feel like you have to do it all. Tell me what is going on.
    - It seems like the workload is having an impact on you — share what's going on for you.
    - What is it like for you right now?
    - What are you doing to create balance and recharge?
* Refocus them on commitments and goals in and out of work
* Help them with prioritizing tasks so they are clear on what to push back on or save for a later date
* Remind them they are part of a team and that you do not expect them to do it all
* Encourage them to work on trusting the team and stakeholders to do their part
* Encourage them to take a few health days off to recharge

ENRAGED

This type of energy can take the appearance of "passive-aggressive" and is usually driven by lack of communication skills and an inability to express one's thoughts and feelings. Many times this person is unsettled or angry about changes at work, volume of work, or type of assignments, and is lacking context between action and big-picture vision.

WHAT YOU CAN DO:

* Initiate an authentic conversation about their state of being
    - I've noticed you've been feeling frustrated. Tell me what is going on.
    - It seems like the workload is having an impact on you – share what's going on for you.
    - Tell me what it is like for you right now.
    - What are you doing to create balance and recharge?
* Refocus them on commitments and goals in and of work
* Ask them open-ended questions about what they are feeling, giving them the chance to express themselves by venting or complaining
* Ask their opinion about issues, so they feel heard and can get clear around the essence of their true complaint or block

SUSTAINABLE ENERGY

Sustainable energy is when individuals are able to sustain or balance energy and they show up as healthfully engaged.

HEALTHFULLY ENGAGED

This type of energy can take the appearance of easy joy and light heartiness, with a positive "We're in this together" attitude. Healthfully engaged people are able to clearly prioritize commitments, have open conversations about demands, and identify stress triggers. They might have peaks of imbalance, but are able to understand the end point and are clear about what they need to do to sustain energy and engagement in those times.

WHAT YOU CAN DO:

- Keep conversation open about balance and their needs/ blocks, as they are constantly changing
  - Keep conversations open about balance and their needs/ blocks, as they are constantly changing:
  - I've noticed you do a great job of finding balance – share with me what you are doing.
  - It seems like you are able to manage the workload really well. How does that feel?
  - Tell me what it is like for you right now.
- Ask them to share best practices with others on the team who are struggling
- Encourage them to keep talking about what they are doing to continue having balance in their life
- Encourage them to take a few health days off to recharge as needed

GET
TALKING

IT'S NOT UP TO MANAGERS TO SOLVE EMPLOYEES' LIFE ISSUES.

HOWEVER, MANAGERS CAN WORK TO EMPOWER THEIR TEAM TO TAKE ACCOUNTABILITY FOR ALL THE CHOICES THEY MAKE THROUGH HAVING MINDFUL CONVERSATIONS.

BEGIN ANYWHERE

There is no right or wrong place to begin practicing mindful management techniques. You can choose to engage in mindful conversations with your team any day, any time, any place.

The practice of mindful management is about choosing to discuss issues you might not even have considered discussing openly with your team until now. The only thing required of you to be a mindful manager is to have these conversations based on what is true for you when it comes to communicating expectations, setting boundaries, and addressing the energy around you.

Starting from a place of personal awareness, a mindful conversation is when you make the content of your message as authentic as possible with clear intent.

By initiating a mindful conversation, you can create intentional, proactive dialog around the pain points associated with workplace imbalance and move your team and organization beyond dealing with tips and tricks to addressing and resolving some of the systemic issues causing imbalance for the team.

There is no way an organization or individual can transform overnight, over a month, or even a over a quarter; these types of individual and organizational behavioral shifts take time.

Being overly aggressive and trying to address and discuss too much, too fast, will likely prove largely unsuccessful. Start where the pain points are the greatest, set boundaries to support or protect your team based on what they need at this point in time, and build from there.

When people at all levels of the organization have better awareness regarding the root causes of imbalance and take accountability for making and accepting choices, the organization can truly begin to shift and evolve toward becoming more connected, conscious, and engaged.

QUESTIONS FOR CLARITY AND CONVERSATION

COMMUNICATE EXPECTATIONS

What does balance mean to you?

What does a leading a balanced team mean to you?

What do you expect from your team?

Team, what do you expect from me?

What do you expect from your manager?

Manager, what do you expect from me?

What do you expect from your company?

How do you expect your team to show up in meetings?

What constitutes a truly urgent request?

When it is a truly urgent issue, how do you expect to be contacted?

What do you expect from your team when they are on vacation?

Are there certain behaviors you expect from your team?

SET BOUNDARIES

What boundaries can you set right now that will help to protect, honor, or uphold team values and commitments?

* Do you expect your team to work weekends?
* What is a reasonable timeframe to reply to email?
* Do you have a preference for where your team works?
* Do you have a preference for when your team works?
* Do you have a preference for how your team wants to be contacted?

What boundaries can you set right now that will help to protect, honor, or uphold your values and commitments?
What is your policy for working on weekends?

* What is a reasonable timeframe to reply to email?
* Do you have a preference for where you work?
* Do you have a preference for when you work?
* Do you have a preference for how your team contacts you?

What is the most comfortable way for you to communicate your boundaries with others? (For example, in writing, face-to-face, one-to-many, or one-on-one?)

What ritual or check-in will you create to remind you to be consistent with living your boundaries and holding boundaries for your team?

How do you know if someone has challenged or disrespected one of your boundaries?

How do you respond when someone has challenged or disrespected one of your boundaries?

ADDRESS ENERGY

What is your energy level right now?

Do you have rituals established to check in with your energy levels?

When your energy level is scarce or abundant, what do you do to shift your energy to be more stable?

Is it possible to create a team ritual to check in on each person's energy levels? What would that look like?

How do you respond when you feel someone's energy in a strong way?

How do you respond when a situation or environment is full of charged energy?

What actions do you take when you need to shift the energy in a room?

How do you begin a conversation with someone whose energy is impacting others?

MAKE A PLAN

It's not up to managers to solve employees' life issues. However, managers can work to empower their team to take accountability for all the choices they make.

Five mindful conversations I am willing to have in the next 30 days

1:

2:

3:

4:

5:

ONE CONVERSATION CAN MAKE A DIFFERENCE.

ONGOING DIALOGUE CAN TRANSFORM A TEAM.

IT DOESN'T MATTER WHERE YOU START —
JUST BEGIN THE CONVERSATION.

THE CHOICE IS YOURS.

MINDFUL THOUGHTS...

MINDFUL THOUGHTS...

MINDFUL THOUGHTS...

MINDFUL THOUGHTS...

MINDLESS THOUGHTS...

ABOUT THE AUTHOR

After years in senior communication roles, working countless hours crafting content for executives at Microsoft, Jae collapsed from stress-related adrenal fatigue directly attributed to the way she was living her life. This life-altering experience propelled Jae deep into research on human behavior, neuroscience, mindfulness, and organizational relationship systems.

In 2008, Jae founded WLB Consulting Group and developed the Mindful Life Program, which includes four group coaching workshops to generate reflection, awareness, and action at the organizational and individual levels.

Jae has taught work-life awareness workshops to thousands of employees at Microsoft and other technology companies in more than 50 countries including China, Russia, India, Japan, Brazil, Argentina, United Arab Emirates, France, Germany, United Kingdom, Norway, Sweden, Canada, and the United States.

Jae has an extensive background in writing and communication with a master's degree in Communication Management from Colorado State University and a bachelor's degree in Broadcast Communication from Metropolitan State College of Denver. She holds certificates in co-active coaching and organizational relationship systems coaching and is the author of seven books.

OTHER BOOKS BY JAE ELLARD

The Five Truths about Work-life Balance is about moving past the misconceptions surrounding work, life, and balance.

The Pocket Coach: Perspective When You Need Some is a book of questions to help you make clear choices.

Success with Stress is about five proactive choices you can make to reduce stress.

THE MINDFUL LIFE COLLECTION

Stop & Think: Creating New Awareness is about the choices you have and the understanding of the impact of the choices you make.

Stop & See: Developing Intentional Habits is about your ability to consciously choose to create habits that support your definitions of balance and success.

Stop & Listen: Practicing Presence is about working with your choices to create deeper engagement with self, others and your environment.

Beyond Tips & Tricks: Mindful Management is about leading groups to take accountability for making and accepting choices.

Created by Jae Ellard

Edited by Jenifer Kooiman

Designed by Hannah Wygal

Beyond Tips and Tricks: Mindful Management, 1st edition

2011-2014 Copyright by Simple Intentions

ISBN 978-0-9828344-7-3

Simple Intentions is a conscious content company working to increase awareness in the workplace. For more information please visit www.simpleintentions.com.

Made in the USA
Charleston, SC
28 October 2015